THE DUKE OF SCHOMBERG
EUROPEAN SOLDIER
WILLIAM'S GENERAL

GORDON LUCY

Schomberg Press
2004

Explorations in Religion, History and Culture
First published in 2004

Schomberg Press
Schomberg House
368 Cregagh Road
Belfast
BT6 9EY
Northern Ireland

ISBN: 0-9547432-0-2
Design by Mark Thompson
Printed by Dorman & Sons Limited

CONTENTS:

'… since it was in our quarrel that he lost his life, we cannot too much honour his memory, which will make a considerable figure in history whilst the world lasts. He was certainly a man of the best education in the world, and knew men and things beyond most of his time, being courteous and civil to everybody and yet had something always that looked so great in him that he commanded respect from men of all qualities and stations. As to his person, he was of middle stature, well proportioned, fair complectioned, a very sound hardy man of his age, and sate an horse the best of any man; he loved constantly to be neat in his clothes, and in his conversation he was always pleasant.'[1]

George Story on the Duke of Schomberg

[1] Story, *A True and Impartial History of the Wars of Ireland* (London, 1691), 85. Story, Williamite historian and Anglican cleric, was the eldest son of Thomas Story of Justice Town, near Carlisle, and in August 1689 he accompanied Schomberg to Ireland as chaplain to Sir Thomas Gower's Regiment of Foot. He was present at the Battle of the Boyne and the siege of Limerick. Between 1694 and 1704 he was Dean of Connor and from 1705 until his death – on 19 November 1721 – he was Dean of Limerick. He is buried in the grounds of St Fethlimidh's Cathedral, Kilmore, County Cavan. *The Dictionary of National Biography* describes Story's *True and Impartial History of the Wars of Ireland* (London, 1691) and his *Continuation of the Impartial History* (London, 1693) as 'by far the most important authority for the war on the Williamite side'. Though his Protestant and Whig sympathies are not in doubt, he endeavoured to live up to the title of his narrative. J. G. Simms described Story's *True and Impartial History* as 'a detailed and relatively objective account'. *Dictionary of National Biography*, xviii, 1314; J. B. Leslie, *Clergy of Connor from Patrician Times to the Present Day* (Belfast, 1993), 614; J. G. Simms *Jacobite Ireland, 1685-91* (London, 1969), 270. Oral information from Mr Winston Heaslip, Kilmore, County Cavan.

Schomberg's career in outline

1615   Born at Heidelberg

1633   Entered the Dutch army

1634   Entered the Swedish army

1635   Transferred to the French army

1639-50   Served in the Dutch army

1652-59   *Maréchal de Camp* and lieutenant-general in the French army

1661-68   Commander of the French and British troops in Portugal

1673   Commander of the British forces for the attack on Walcheren

1673-74   Created duke and commanded French army in Rousillon

1675   Marshal of France

1685   Went to Portugal after the Revocation of the Edict of Nantes

1687   Entered the service of Brandenburg-Prussia

1688   Second-in-command of William of Orange's invasion of England

1689   Commander of Williamite expedition to Ireland

1690   Killed at the Battle of the Boyne

The Duke of Schomberg

INTRODUCTION

The fame of the Duke of Schomberg, or Marshal Schomberg, does not even begin to match that of William of Orange, Schomberg's royal master for the last three years of his long life. Indeed, few would attempt to argue that Schomberg is a household name in modern Ulster.

His death at the Battle of the Boyne is depicted on a few Orange banners, while others portray him welcoming William at Carrickfergus or leaving Hillsborough with the King on their way to the Boyne. A painting by Jan Wyck in the Ulster Museum traditionally said to depict the death of Schomberg has, in the absence of evidence to support this contention, been re-catalogued as representing a cavalry skirmish of the day. It is rarely, if ever on display. A similar painting in the National Gallery of Ireland in Dublin – also originally said to depict the death of Schomberg but also re-catalogued as representing a cavalry skirmish – provided the image for the front cover of Brendan Fitzpatrick's volume covering the seventeenth century in the New Gill History of Ireland series in 1988.[2]

In Belfast Schomberg is commemorated by Schomberg Avenue, Schomberg Drive, Schomberg Park and Schomberg Street. The Avenue and the Park are in Belmont in east Belfast and take their name from Schomberg House, the home for many years of various members of the Ewart family, a family of Belfast linen barons. The Drive and the Street are in Sandy Row in the south of the city and the heartland – in the eyes of Sandy Row folk – of Belfast Orangeism. In January 2001 the Orange Institution moved its headquarters from the House of Orange in Dublin Road to the Cregagh Road, calling its new headquarters Schomberg House. Schomberg has also been commemorated by the formation of the Schomberg Society, a cultural society which has been developed around a fife and drum band, in Kilkeel, County Down.

---

[2] Brendan Fitzpatrick, *Seventeenth-Century Ireland: The Wars of Religion* (Dublin, 1988).

Although this introductory publication is not a conventional biographical study, it does seek to provide the basic facts about Schomberg's career. It also examines a number of topics relevant to Schomberg's own experience: what it meant to be a soldier of fortune; the fate of the Huguenots, whose Reformed faith Schomberg shared, in Louis XIV's France; and the 'Glorious Revolution' and Schomberg's role as William of Orange's second-in-command in the invasion of England. Events in Ireland – more specifically, the background to Schomberg's Irish campaign, the campaign itself, his death at the Boyne, and his contribution to William's victory – form the core of the publication.

Duke of Schomberg Flute Band, Donaghadee, County Down, 12 July 2004

Schomberg's True Blues, Donaghadee, County Down, 12 July 2004

The Duke of Schomberg

1: THE DUKE OF SCHOMBERG

FRIEDRICH HERMANN VON SCHÖNBERG *is better known in the English-speaking-world as the Duke of Schomberg.[3] As his name suggests, Schomberg was German by birth but he was a cosmopolitan figure who became a soldier of fortune, a marshal of France and an English peer. He fought in the service of various countries in most of the major European conflicts between 1634 and 1690. Being multilingual, he was especially skilled at commanding forces of mixed national origin. Along with Revd Dr George Walker, the former Governor of Londonderry and Bishop-designate of Derry, he was one of the two most notable casualties at the Battle of the Boyne on 1 July 1690.*

The only son of Hans Meinhard von Schönberg, the Court Marshal of Frederick V, Elector Palatine, and of Anne, daughter of an English peer, the 5th Lord Dudley; the future Duke was born on 16 December 1615 at Heidelberg, in the Palatinate (south-western Germany). His mother died giving birth to her son. Nine months later his father died, leaving the young Schomberg an orphan before he had reached his first birthday.[4] His paternal grandmother, Dorothea Riedsal von Bellersheim, assumed responsibility for his upbringing and so he grew up in the United Provinces (the Netherlands).

Still under twenty, he volunteered for military service under Frederick Henry of Orange in 1633 and, from 1634 to 1637 during the Thirty Years War, he served in the army of Bernard of Saxe-Weimar in the campaigns on the upper Rhine. In 1639 he again went to Holland, serving with the Dutch army for several years.

---

[3] Armand-Fréderic de Schomberg in French.
[4] Arguably, the most historically significant achievement of Schomberg's father was negotiating the marriage of Frederick V to Elizabeth, daughter of James I of England and VI of Scots and the future William III's great-aunt. John Carswell, *The Descent on England: A Study of the English Revolution of 1688 & Its European Background* (London, 1969), 19.

In 1650, during the crisis known as the *Fronde*,[5] Cardinal Mazarin, secured Schomberg and his German infantry for the French royal army that defeated the rebel Marshal de Turenne at the Battle of Rethel on 15 December 1650. Schomberg was appointed *Maréchal de camp* on 28 October 1652, and, after Turenne had changed sides, became one of Turenne's best officers in the campaigns against Spain and the Prince de Condé.[6]

A decade later, in 1660, Schomberg was called to Lisbon to organize the Portuguese army when Spain was threatening to terminate Portugal's 20 years of independence. In June 1663 Sancho Manuel, Count of Vila Flor, defeated Don John of Austria at Ameixial, and in June 1665 Schomberg won the important victory of Montes Claros. Schomberg also placed Dom Pedro (later Pedro II) in power after a palace revolution in 1668.[7] Peace was finally made by the Treaty of Lisbon in the course of the same year and Spain at last recognized Portuguese independence. Schomberg returned to his position in the French army, having become naturalised as a Frenchman in 1664.

In 1673, during the Dutch War (1672-78), Schomberg went to England on the invitation of Charles II to form an army for the proposed invasion of Holland. However he soon returned to the French Army and was on Louis XIV's staff at the siege and capture of Maastricht in June 1673. Schomberg was most emphatically not William's general at this stage: they were opponents. Indeed, Schomberg succeeded in outmanoeuvring William

---

[5] During the minority of Louis XIV of France, between 1638 and 1651, there were revolts, called the *Frondes*, against the government of Cardinal Mazarin, the chief minister, and the regent, Louis's mother, Anne of Austria, in 1648-9 and 1650. The term *Fronde* is derived from the 'sling' of a children's game played in the streets of Paris in defiance of the civil authorities. See 'The Frondes', in E. N. Williams, *The Penguin Dictionary of English and European History, 1485-1789* (Harmondsworth, 1980), 175-6.
[6] See 'Turenne' in Anthony Livesey, *The Battles of the Great Commanders* (London, 1990), 60-7. There is also a brief piece on the Prince de Condé, Turenne's principal opponent in the Battle of the Dunes, 14 June 1658, 66.
[7] Revisionist historians – including perhaps Karl Marx – might see a parallel between Schomberg's role in events in Portugal in 1668 and his role in events in England in 1688. Marx contended that the 'Glorious Revolution' of 1688 was no more than a palace coup. He also claimed that William of Orange was the instrument of the bourgeoisie and the agent of foreign policies based on commercial interests. See Eveline Cruickshanks, *The Glorious Revolution* (Basingstoke, 2000), 96.

of Orange at least twice during the early 1670s: in 1674 he elegantly avoided William's attempt to cut him off from the main French force and in 1676, though inferior in numbers, he forced William to raise his siege of Maastricht.[8] In the latter half of 1674 Schomberg commanded a small French force in Roussillon (in the Pyrennes) and repulsed the Spanish. The following year he was one of eight *Maréchals de France* appointed on Turenne's death. Arguably, Schomberg's marshal's baton was reward for – and recognition of – his military prowess and skill against William.[9]

Louis II de Bourbon, Prince de Condé, Seventeenth-century mercenary commander

[8] Padráig Lenihan, 1690: *Battle of the Boyne* (Stroud, 2003), 94-5.
[9] For a much fuller account of Schomberg's life, see 'Schomberg' in Leslie Stephens & Sidney Lee (eds), *Dictionary of National Biography*, xvii (Oxford, 1922-3), 913-21.

Prince Maurice of Nassau

2: BEING A MERCENARY

Schomberg was a soldier of fortune or a mercenary. The Greeks and the Romans employed mercenaries.[10] From the earliest days of organized warfare until the emergence of standing armies in the mid-seventeenth century, governments frequently supplemented their military forces with mercenaries.

To describe someone today as mercenary is not a compliment. A mercenary may be defined as a hired professional soldier who fights for any state or nation, usually, but not always, without regard to political interests or issues. Just as a lawyer, a doctor or any other professional provides a service to his (or, these days, her) client or patient in return for a fee, a mercenary was a professional – his profession being that of a soldier – who was prepared to offer his services in return for payment.

Seventeenth-century commanders changed allegiance without inhibition. For example, Louis II de Bourbon, Prince de Condé, at one stage served Louis XIV of France, then Philip IV of Spain, before reverting to his original allegiance. Turenne was a son of the Protestant Henri, Duc de Bouillon, by his second wife, Elizabeth of Nassau, daughter of William the Silent, the Stadholder of the Netherlands. When his father died in 1623, Turenne was sent to learn soldiering with his mother's brothers, Maurice and Frederick Henry, the Princes of Orange who were leading the Dutch against Spain in the Netherlands. Though he was given command of an infantry regiment in French service for the campaign of 1630, he was back with Frederick Henry in 1632.

---

[10] Xenophon (431 BC to c. 350 BC), the Greek historian is perhaps the ancient world's most famous mercenary. He served with the Greek mercenaries of the Persian prince Cyrus, first as a soldier of fortune and then, after Cyrus's death, as an elected commander of the Greek force, the 'Ten Thousand', composed of men who found themselves 1,000 miles from home and who fought their way through the unknown territories of Kurdistan and Armenia until they reached the Greek city of Trapezus (now Trabzon) on the Black Sea early in 400 BC. This exploit provided the basis of *Anabasis Kyrou* (literally, 'The Upcountry March' but usually entitled in English, 'The Ten Thousand') which secured him his reputation and his fortune. See Melanie Parry, *Chambers Biographical Dictionary*, 6th ed. (Edinburgh 1997), 1987.

Lieutenant-Colonel Lawrence Dempsey provides a less exalted local example. In June 1690 as William III advanced south towards the Boyne there was a minor skirmish at the Moyry pass (also known as the Gap of the North) between Newry and Dundalk, where a small force of Jacobites harassed the Williamite army.

As is frequently the case, accounts differ as to the precise detail. Colonel Thomas Bellingham, a Williamite officer, thought his side lost about 20 men but the Jacobites suffered greater casualties. John Stevens, an English Jacobite officer, candidly admitted that he was not present but according to the account he obtained from those who were, the Jacobites had a 'few wounded and fewer killed' in the confrontation. However, among the Jacobite casualties was Dempsey who was shot in the shoulder and died of his wounds. Dempsey had served under Schomberg in Portugal.[11]

Mercenaries had an often-deserved reputation for being greedy, brutal, and undisciplined. They were capable of deserting on the eve of battle, betraying their patrons, and plundering civilians. Much of their mutinous behaviour was the result of their employers' unwillingness or inability to pay for their services.[12] When rigid discipline, sustained by prompt payment, was enforced (as in the army of Maurice of Nassau), mercenaries could prove to be extremely effective soldiers.[13]

During the Thirty Years War (1618-48) some 25,000 Scots – almost ten per cent of the country's adult male population – went abroad to serve as soldiers, mostly in the service of Protestant states. Alexander Hamilton raised a regiment, 800 strong, to fight for Gustavus Adolphus of Sweden in 1631.[14]

[11] Lenihan, *1690: Battle of the Boyne,* 172. For an account of the skirmish, see also Richard Doherty, *The Williamite War in Ireland,* 1688-1691 (Dublin, 1998), 107.

[12] Geoffrey Parker, 'Mutiny and Discontent in the Spanish Army of Flanders, 1572-1607' in Geoffrey Parker, *Spain and the Netherlands,* 1559-1659 (Glasgow, 1979), 106-121.

[13] Geoffrey Parker, 'The "Military Revolution, 1560-1660" – a Myth?' in Parker, *Spain and the Netherlands,* 86-103.

[14] Geoffrey Parker, 'Dynastic Warfare, 1494-1660' in Geoffrey Parker (ed), *The Cambridge Illustrated History of Warfare* (Cambridge, 1995), 149.

Robert Monro, the commander of the Scottish Covenanting army in Ulster which suffered defeated at the hands of Owen Roe O'Neill at the Battle of Benburb on 5 June 1646, had served with the Swedish army in Germany with fellow-Scots between 1627 and 1633. Monro also has the distinction of being the author of the first regimental history written in English: *Monro: his Expedition with the Worthy Scots Regiment called Mackays.*[15] In his book Monro sought to explain his motivation for fighting in Europe. Monro admitted to a desire for travel and adventure, and for military experience under an illustrious leader but, interestingly, he placed above these motives the desire to defend the Protestant faith and the claims and the honour of Elizabeth Stuart, his king's sister and the widow of the 'Winter King'.[16]

Swiss soldiers were hired out on a large scale all over Europe by their own cantonal governments and enjoyed a high reputation. Since 1506 the Papal Swiss Guards have been responsible for the safety of the pontiff and have served as his personal escort. In eighteenth-century France Swiss regiments were the elite formations of the regular army. During the American War of Independence the British government employed Hessian mercenaries to fight the rebellious colonists.[17]

Since the late eighteenth century, however, mercenaries have been, for the most part, individual soldiers of fortune. The French and Spanish Foreign Legions and the Gurkhas of Nepal are conspicuous exceptions.[18] The Gurkhas, famous for their fighting qualities, have served with the British army since the mid-nineteenth century and since 1947 have been a significant minority within the army of India. Nearly 10,000 Gurkhas serve in British Gurkha units and 50,000 in Indian Gurkha units. The British maintain a recruiting centre at Dharan.

Nepal's Gurkha veterans are a valuable human resource. Upon returning home, many of them become teachers and community leaders, bringing new ideas and technology to the mountain regions.

---

[15] Geoffrey Parker, 'Dynastic Warfare, 1494-1660', 160.
[16] Geoffrey Parker (ed), *The Thirty Years War* (London, 1984), 195.
[17] See Hugh Bicheno, *Rebels and Redcoats: The American Revolutionary War* (London, 2003).
[18] See Martin Windrow, *French Foreign Legion, 1914-1945* (Oxford, 1996) and Mike Chappell, *The Gurkhas* (Oxford, 1996).

Admiral Gaspard de Coligny, the leader of the Huguenots

3: THE HUGUENOTS AND THE REVOCATION OF THE EDICT OF NANTES [19]

As a naturalized Frenchman and a Protestant, Schomberg may be regarded as a Huguenot, the term used to describe French Protestants. The origin of the term is obscure but it is alleged to come from the word **aignos**, *derived from the German* **Eidgenossen** *(confederates bound together by oath).[20] Huguenots were usually but not always Calvinists. Jean (John) Calvin was French, even though he is invariably associated primarily with Geneva rather than France.[21]*

France was initially slow to respond to the message of the Reformation but by the 1540s progress was becoming rapid, especially in the towns. With the conspicuous exception of the Cévennes (the south-east edge of the Massif Central), rural French people tended to be less receptive to Protestantism.[22] French Protestantism's early leaders were to be found among the regular clergy, especially the mendicant orders. Their earliest followers were mostly artisans and small tradesmen. Protestantism's appeal then extended up the social ladder to attract notaries, doctors and local office-holders.[23]

---

[19] The tercentenary of the Revocation of the Edict of Nantes in 1985 occasioned the publication of a great deal of interesting material on the Huguenots. Two books were especially useful in writing this section: Robin D. Gwynn, *Huguenot Heritage: The History and Contribution of the Huguenots in Britain* (London, 1985) and C. E. J. Caldicott, H. Gough & J-P Pittion (eds), *The Huguenots and Ireland: Anatomy of an Emigration* (Dun Laoghaire, 1987). Jean-Paul Pittion, 'The French Protestants and the Edict of Nantes (1549-1685): a chronology based on material in Marsh's Library in Dublin', 37-66, in the latter volume is fascinating. Marsh's Library, built in 1701 by Archbishop Marsh (1638-1713), the Church of Ireland Archbishop of Dublin, was the first public library in Ireland. Dr Elias Bouhéreau, the first librarian, was a Huguenot refugee who fled from France in 1695. See www.marshlibrary.ie

[20] Gwynn, Huguenot Heritage, 2.

[21] Calvin was born in Noyon, Picardy, in 1509. Parry, *Chambers Biographical Dictionary,* 323.

[22] Robin Briggs, *Early Modern France, 1560-1715* (Oxford, 1977), 13.

[23] Briggs, *Early Modern France,* 12.

Eventually, it reached the French nobility, often beginning with the women who then won over their husbands and sons.[24]

The 1550s were also years of considerable progress for French Protestantism. Life, however, became very difficult for the Huguenots when the authorities feared that France might become a Protestant country. Accordingly, François I (1515-47) and Henri II (1547-59) viciously persecuted the Huguenots. The Massacre of St Bartholomew's Day on 24 August 1572, in which perhaps 2,000 French Protestants perished, was a serious attempt on the part of Catherine de Medici, the Regent of France, to exterminate the leadership of French Protestantism. The massacre's most notable victim was Admiral Gaspard de Coligny, the Huguenot leader.[25] The Huguenots then endured the religious wars of the next thirty years. However, on 13 April 1598 Henri IV (a former Huguenot who had decided that 'Paris' – that is to say, the French crown – 'was worth a mass') granted his former co-religionists toleration under the Edict of Nantes. The Edict also signalled the end of the sixteenth-century Wars of Religion in France.[26]

The Edict allowed Protestants to worship privately in the houses of great nobles and publicly in the towns designated by the earlier Treaty of Poitiers, with one or two additions in each judicial district. Protestants could hold synods from time to time and were to enjoy equality with Roman Catholics in access to public office and education. Protestants were to control the universities of La Rochelle, Nîmes and Montauban. Special courts were to

[24] By the 1560s perhaps as much as half the French aristocracy had embraced Protestantism, compared to a conversion rate at large of 10 to 20 per cent. J. H. Elliott, *Europe Divided, 1559-1598* (Glasgow, 1968), 96.
[25] Elliott, *Europe Divided*, 215-25.
[26] Because the revocation of the Edict of Nantes was clearly a 'bad thing' – as Sellar and Yeatman might have observed had they written a companion volume on European history to sit alongside *1066 and All That* – there is an automatic assumption that the Edict of Nantes was a 'good thing'. As Gwynn points out, however, the Huguenots paid an extremely high price for the peace and the security which the Edict afforded them. They were obliged to abandon all hope of missionary expansion, Protestant churches and schools were allowed only in certain locations, and Protestant books could only be printed and publicly sold in Protestant towns. The Edict effectively placed French Protestantism in a straitjacket. Furthermore, the protection which Protestants enjoyed under the terms of the Edict was wholly dependent on the continuance of royal favour. Gwynn, *Huguenot Heritage*, 19.

Henry IV and the captulation of Paris. "Well worth a mass"

be set up in the *parlements* of Paris, Toulouse, Bordeaux and Grenoble to try cases in which Protestants were involved. Finally, Protestants were allowed to hold about 100 strongholds, or *places de sûreté*, for eight years, the expense of garrisoning them being met by the king.

Nevertheless, religious conflict erupted again in the 1620s during the reign of Louis XIII (1610-43). Eventually the Huguenots were defeated and the Peace of Alès was signed on 28 June 1629. Under its terms the Huguenots were allowed to retain their freedom of conscience but lost most of their political and military privileges. No longer 'a state within a state', the Huguenots became loyal subjects of the king. Before the Massacre of St. Bartholomew's Day Jean Calvin had advocated obedience to the civil magistrate, that is, to royal authority. After the Massacre this doctrine was rendered clearly untenable and Huguenots had asserted their right to rebel against the king if he would not guarantee them toleration. However, on being re-granted religious toleration, Huguenots were more than happy to be loyal subjects.[27] Their remaining rights under the Edict of Nantes were confirmed by a royal declaration in 1643 on behalf of the infant Louis XIV (1643-1715).

However, the French Roman Catholic clergy could not accept toleration for the Huguenots and worked to deprive them of their remaining rights. The clergy's influence was deployed to persuade Louis that toleration was not a virtue and that unity in the state was threatened where two or more Churches were tolerated.[28]

---

[27] Gwynn, *Huguenot Heritage*, 20.
[28] However, Innocent XI, the outstanding pope of the seventeenth century in terms of both character and ability, opposed Louis's persecution of the Huguenots because he believed that toleration was desirable, not least in order to maintain peace in Europe. Innocent XI was elected pope in 1676 in the face of fierce opposition from Louis XIV. On most issues Innocent XI opposed Louis, so much so that Innocent was favourably disposed to William of Orange. Innocent died on 12 August 1689 at Rome. Had Innocent lived to see William III's victory at the Boyne a year later he might well have rejoiced at the news. Certainly, William's victory was warmly welcomed in Madrid and *Te Deums* were sung in the cathedrals of Roman Catholic Austria for the success of the Emperor's Protestant ally. Innocent's successor, Alexander VIII, was conspicuously less hostile to France and was appalled by the response in Austria to William's victory. The oft-repeated assertion that the pope was on King William's side at the Battle of the Boyne fails to take account of the change of pontiff in 1689. See Parry, *Chambers Biographical Dictionary*, 954.

Louis began interpreting the terms of the Edict as narrowly as possible. Everything not expressly in the Edict – including the Reformed Church's annual Synod, new church buildings and daytime burials of the dead – was forbidden. All Protestant churches erected after 1598 were pulled down (by 1685 only 243 remained out of an original 813). A fund was established in 1677 to buy conversions. General harassment and the forcible conversion of thousands of Protestants, vigorously pursued for many years, were intensified. Huguenots were excluded from public office, barred from the legal profession, could not practise medicine and could not print or sell books. The movements of ministers were controlled. Ministers were even forbidden to visit the dying. Protestant children were taken away from their parents and brought up as Roman Catholics.[29] The notorious practice of *dragonnades*, the billeting of soldiers on Protestant families with permission to behave as brutally as they wished, was introduced in Upper and Middle Poitou in 1681. The policy was then extended to Dauphiné and Vivaris and was subsequently employed in Béarn and in the Languedoc.[30] Finally, on 18 October 1685 Louis XIV promulgated the Edict of Fontainebleau which revoked what was left of the Edict of Nantes. Religious toleration was thereby brought to an end in France. Henceforward, Protestantism was illegal in the land of Calvin's birth. The Huguenot population was forcibly converted to Roman Catholicism. Despite the fact that emigration was illegal, between 200,000 and 400,000 Huguenots fled France, taking their invaluable skills and expertise, especially in industry and commerce, with them. France's loss was the wider world's gain.[31] Many emigrated to England, Ulster (especially to the Lisburn area), the rest of Ireland, Prussia, the Netherlands, America and the Cape of Good Hope and became very useful citizens of their adopted countries.[32]

What was Schomberg's attitude to the persecution of the Huguenots? Schomberg was himself a staunch Protestant. In 1674-75, while in French service, he came under criticism for allowing the troops under his command

[29] Gwynn, 'An Exposed Minority', *Huguenot Heritage,* 6-25, especially 21-2.
[30] Pittion, 'The French Protestants and Edict of Nantes', 52.
[31] Gwynn, *Huguenot Heritage,* 144-5.
[32] G. Elmore Reaman, *The Trail of the Huguenots in Europe, the United States, South Africa, and Canada* (Baltimore, MD, 1986).

religious toleration.[33] When Schomberg was awarded his marshal's baton in 1675 Louis XIV sanctioned a clumsy effort to woo him away from his Protestant faith. Turenne, with his impeccable Protestant parentage – he was after all the grandson of William the Silent – offered an encouraging precedent. In April 1660 when Turenne was appointed 'marshal-general of the camps and armies of the King', the prospect of becoming Constable of France (i.e. *ex officio* commander-in- chief in war) was dangled before him. In 1668, after the death of Charlotte de Caumont, his firmly Protestant wife, Turenne converted to Roman Catholicism. However, it was to no avail for he was never made Constable of France. Louis, however, clearly misjudged Schomberg. Schomberg, in conversation with Henry Sidney, the English politician, in February 1680, alluded to his increasing dissatisfaction with developments in France and indicated that he would gladly live somewhere else.[34]

After the revocation of the Edict of Nantes, Schomberg did indeed leave France although he did not flee the country. Given Schomberg's European reputation Louis permitted him to go to Portugal under the pretext of a diplomatic mission and, as a special concession, allowed him to retain his French properties and pensions.[35] However, his departure from France was clearly prompted by his disapproval of the persecution of the Huguenots.

In Portugal both Pedro II, the Portuguese monarch, and the French ambassador to Lisbon made every effort to persuade Schomberg to abandon his faith and embrace Roman Catholicism. While Schomberg listened politely to what they had to say he gave them no encouragement. Not only were their efforts unavailing, they proved counterproductive.

In November 1685 Frederick William of Brandenburg, 'the Great Elector' and the uncle of William of Orange, had responded to the Edict of Fontainebleau with the Edict of Potsdam which offered the Huguenots shelter in Brandenburg-Prussia. In January 1687 Schomberg, weary of the proselytising of Pedro and the French ambassador, decided to accept Frederick William's

[33] 'Schomberg' in Leslie Stephens & Sidney Lee (eds), *DNB*, xvii (Oxford, 1922-3), 917.
[34] 'Schomberg' in Stephens & Lee (eds), *DNB*, xvii, 918.
[35] 'Schomberg' in Stephens & Lee (eds), *DNB*, xvii, 918.

offer of shelter and travelled to Berlin via the Dutch Republic. In return Frederick William showered him with gifts, appointing him a privy councillor and commander-in-chief of his army.[36] Schomberg was not alone: according to Marshal Vauban, the outstanding French military engineer of the era, about 500 or 600 Huguenot officers and some 10,000 to 12,000 Huguenot troops fled France and entered the service of England, Holland and various German states, including Brandenburg-Prussia.[37] Not surprisingly Louis XIV's France had few foes more bitter than the Huguenots.

In September 1688 Frederick III, the successor to 'the Great Elector', despatched Schomberg and an army to occupy Cologne in a bid to forestall Louis XIV's attempts to interfere in the filling of the vacancy created by the death of the Archbishop-Elector of the archdiocese. In retaliation Louis XIV confiscated Schomberg's French properties.

The murder of Admiral Gaspard de Coligny, the Huguenot leader. On 22 August 1572 Coligny had only narrowly escaped assassination. Two days later - on St Bartholomew's Day - two assassins burst into his bedroom, struck down the already wounded Coligny and hurled his body into the street through the window

[36] 'Schomberg' in Stephens & Lee (eds), *DNB*, xvii, 918.
[37] Gwynn, *Huguenot Heritage*, 145.

Willem van Oranje: Prince of Orange, Count of Nassau-Dillenburg,
Stadholder of the United Provinces and future King of England, Scotland and Ireland

4: THE "GLORIOUS REVOLUTION"

The 'Glorious Revolution' is the name given by Whig historians to the events of 1688-89 that resulted in the abdication of James II and the succession of William III and Mary II. 'Glorious' is usually regarded as a commentary on the fact that in England the Revolution involved the shedding of very little blood. In Scotland and Ireland, however, there was significant bloodshed. In Ireland, the Revolution was the prelude to the Williamite War.

The consequences of the 'Glorious Revolution' were indeed glorious. In *1688: A Global History* (2001) John E. Wills, the American historian, provides an international appreciation of the significance of the events of 1688-89. Acknowledging that the Revolution was 'almost completely bloodless', Wills makes the point that it was also glorious in that

> it opened up the way to the various forms of constitutional government we cherish today. The Declaration of Rights of 1689 established an elected Parliament as supreme in the fundamentals of taxation and legislation and set clear limits to royal power. These beginnings were elaborated on in subsequent centuries not only by parliamentary governments of English heritage in London, Ottawa, New Delhi, and elsewhere but also by parliamentary regimes of varied language and much more mixed lineage in Paris, Prague, and Tokyo and by the non-parliamentary government of the United States.[38]

In allowing William to invade England, Louis XIV of France massively miscalculated. Louis assumed that James II would be resolute in defence of his crown and that William would be tied down in a protracted campaign in England. Thus, in September 1688 Louis felt able to invade and lay waste to the Palatinate, Schomberg's homeland, in order to press the rights of his sister-in-law and to besiege Philippsburg, a fortress on the Rhine, in order to advance the claims of Wilhelm von Fürstenburg, the Bishop of Strasbourg and Louis's protégé, to the vacant archbishopric of Cologne.

---

[38] John E. Wills, *1688: A Global History* (London, 2001), 183.

William had been in clandestine contact with various leading English politicians and with army and naval officers hostile to James's policies. At the end of June 1688 William was invited by four Whigs, two Tories and Bishop Compton of London to intervene in order to prevent James from promoting the interests of Roman Catholicism, expanding the army and purging it of Protestants, and manipulating elections to the Parliament that was scheduled to meet in November. The birth of an infant prince to Mary Beatrice of Modena, James's wife, on 10 June, had transformed the political future, holding out the prospect of a Roman Catholic dynasty. The son – James Edward, better known to history as 'the Old Pretender' – would succeed James and would exclude Mary, James's eldest, Protestant daughter, married to William of Orange, from the throne. Many people were persuaded that the child was 'suppositious': somebody else's baby concealed in a warming pan and smuggled into the Queen's bedchamber to give the appearance of a royal birth.

Serious military intervention was necessary because of the size of James's professional army, even though William was promised that most of its officers would defect. William needed a reliable second-in-command. Schomberg had a European reputation and was well known and respected in England. In Macaulay's words, Schomberg

> was regarded by all Protestants as a confessor who had endured everything for the truth. For his religion he had resigned a splendid income, had lain down the truncheon of a Marshal of France, and had begun the world again as a needy soldier of fortune.[39]

Despite being in his seventies Schomberg seemed to William to be the best possible choice, not least because of his experience in commanding forces of mixed national origin. With the approval of the Elector of Brandenburg, Schomberg and his two sons visited Holland to meet William and to receive instructions on 22 July 1688 to prepare for 'the descent on England'. The Elector also lent him troops for the enterprise.

---

[39] Thomas Babington Macaulay, *The History of England* (London: Folio Press, 1986) iii, 315-6.

William and Schomberg assembled an army of at least 20,000 men, including a high proportion of his battle-hardened Dutch veterans. Some accounts suggest a force twice this size.[40]

They also assembled 5,000 horses for the cavalry and 2,000 draught animals to pull artillery and heavy equipment. William's taskforce was to be conveyed to England in a flotilla of almost 500 ships. Although assured of English support once he landed, William's plans did not depend on it. William's operation was intended to be self-sufficient.

There was a day of fasting and prayer throughout the United Provinces for the success of William's great venture on 17 October. In Haarlem prayers were said in the Reformed, French Calvinist, Remonstrant, Lutheran and Mennonite Churches. In the magnificent Portuguese Synagogue in Amsterdam there was a special prayer calling on the God of Israel to

> bless, guard, favour, support, save, exalt, enhance, and raise to the most glittering peak of success the Noble and Mighty States of Holland and West-Friesland, the High and Mighty States General of the United Provinces, and His Highness the Prince of Orange, Stadholder and Captain-General by sea and land of these provinces, with all their allies, and the noble and illustrious burgomasters and magistracy of this city of Amsterdam. [41]

William's formidable invasion fleet first set sail from Den Briel, near Rotterdam, on 20 October in fine weather but encountered such a severe storm that the fleet was scattered. Barrels broke loose and rolled around below decks and perhaps as many as 1,300 horses were killed, suffocated below battened down hatches or as a result of having their skulls smashed against the sides of the ships. William's flagship was almost wrecked. The fleet was obliged to return to various Dutch ports. Although only one ship had been lost in the storm, the loss of so many horses was a serious blow. When Gilbert Burnet, William's chaplain and the future Bishop of Salisbury, who had been on the same ship as William, gloomily observed that it seemed predestined that they should not set foot on English soil, William made no reply. [42]

[40] For example, Eveline Cruickshanks asserts that William's taskforce consisted of 40,000 troops, a force greater than the Spanish Armada in 1588. She also suggests that William's force was twice the size of James's army which was dispersed throughout the British Isles. Cruickshanks, *The Glorious Revolution*, 26.
[41] John E. Wills, *1688: A Global History*, 215.
[42] Henri & Barbara van der Zee, *William and Mary* (London, 1973), 250.

William was not so easily disheartened nor was he about to give up on his great enterprise. All the damage was made good with incredible speed and he set sail again on 2 November. On 3 November the Dutch fleet sailed with all flags flying through the Straits of Dover with crowds watching from the cliffs on both sides of the Channel. From the mast of *Den Briel*, William's flagship, streamed a banner with the motto of the House of Orange: *'Je Maintiendrai'*. From the masts of other ships streamed banners with mottos such as *'Pro libertate et religione'* and *'Pro religione protestante'*.

On 5 November – the day after William's 38th birthday and the exact anniversary of the Gunpowder Plot – William's fleet dropped anchor at Torbay. [43] Count Solms, one of William's commanders, was rowed ashore by ten grenadiers, and encountered no resistance from the people of Brixham. Shortly afterwards William followed Solms ashore. Recognising him, some local women rushed into the sea to kiss his hands, saying 'God bless you!' William and Schomberg observed the disembarkation of their troops. A relaxed and unusually happy William greeted Dr Burnet, when he came ashore, with the words, 'What do you think of Predestination now, Doctor?' [44]

In invading England, William and Schomberg succeeded in doing what Philip II of Spain, Napoleon and Hitler failed to do. Success was by no means a foregone conclusion. The logistical problems were formidable. Henry Tudor, the future Henry VII, had mounted the last successful seaborne invasion of Britain, landing at Milford Haven in south Wales on 7 August 1485 and defeating Richard III at Bosworth on 22 August. More recent history did not offer much encouragement. Monmouth's rebellion three years earlier offered a cautionary tale. However, Monmouth had been a rank amateur. William and Schomberg were professional soldiers who did not fail to plan but planned meticulously to succeed. They succeeded in evading the English navy (although it might be more accurate to observe that the English navy evaded

---

[43] At William's suggestion, the annual service of thanksgiving for deliverance from the Gunpowder Plot on 5 November was amended to include thanks for the 'happy arrival' of the Prince of Orange and 'the Deliverance of our Church and Nation'. Cruickshanks, *Glorious Revolution*, 40-1.
[44] Van der Zee, *William and Mary*, 253. Macaulay observes: 'The reproof was so delicate that Burnet … did not perceive it'. Macaulay, *History of England*, ii, 368.

An Exact

DIARY

OF THE

Late Expedition

OF

His Illustrious Highness

THE

Prince of Orange,

(Now KING of *Great Britain*)

From his Palace at the *HAGUE*,

To his Landing at *TORBAY*;

And from thence

To his Arrival at *WHITE-HALL*.

Giving a particular ACCOUNT

Of all that happened, and every Day's March.

By a Minister, Chaplain in the ARMY.

LONDON:

Printed for *Richard Baldwin*, near the *Black Bull* in the

Old-Baily. MDCLXXXIX.

William lands at Torbay

2 1

them) and in making an unopposed landing. Amphibious operations are notoriously difficult: confronting James's large standing army at Brixham would have been a hazardous undertaking.[45]

As William's second-in-command, Schomberg rode into Exeter on 9 November at William's side. William, in highly-polished armour, mounted on a white horse, entered the city with an escort consisting of 300 cavalry impressively mounted on Flanders horses; 200 'Negroes from Surinam', colourfully attired in embroidered capes lined with fur and plumes of white feathers on their heads; 200 Laplanders in black armour with reindeer skins over their shoulders and armed with broadswords; his banner, supported by 100 gentlemen and pages; and by 500 warhorses, each led by two grooms. William was followed by another contingent of 200 cavalry, 3,000 Swiss mercenaries, the first 500 English volunteers, each leading two horses, and 600 of William's famous Dutch Blue Guards in full armour. The rest of the army, thousands of common soldiers, and 21 enormous cannon, each one pulled by 16 carthorses, brought up the rear. It was a spectacle intended to inspire awe.

As the Bishop and Dean had fled the city, Dr Burnet organised a solemn service of thanksgiving in Exeter Cathedral. The nervous canons stayed away but the choristers and prebendaries were present until, after the *Te Deum,* William's Declaration was read, at which point they left hurriedly. Dr Burnet concluded the service with the words, 'God Save the Prince of Orange'. Not everyone responded, 'Amen!'

The common people extended to William a warm if somewhat cautious welcome. As one individual explained to Constantyn Huygens, 'If this thing do miscarry we are all undone'.[46]

---

[45] Writing about early-nineteenth century amphibious operations, Charles Esdaile observes 'setting aside the dangers of storms and shipwreck, transporting even the most modest expeditionary force required large numbers of specialist ships, whilst simply getting the forces involved on and off ship was a most complex undertaking'. Charles Esdaile, *The Peninsular War* (London, 2002), 3. The Dardanelles campaign of April 1915 to January 1916 offers a stunning twentieth-century exemplar of how ill-conceived and inadequately equipped amphibious operations are doomed to disaster. See Nigel Steel and Peter Hart, *Defeat at Gallipoli* (London, 1994).
[46] Van der Zee, *William and Mary,* 253.

The common people were haunted by the recent memory of the 'Bloody Assizes' conducted by Judge Jeffreys after Monmouth's defeat at the Battle of Sedgemoor in July 1685. More than 300 supporters of Monmouth had been executed. At least a further 800 had been transported to the West Indies. The brutal and vindictive Jeffreys boasted, with a degree of hyperbole, that he had hanged more men than all the judges of England since William the Conqueror.

'The Great and the Good' were even more cautious than the common people. The authors of the Invitation of June 1688, asking William to intervene in the affairs of England, had promised to rally to him when he arrived. As yet, to William's intense displeasure, they had exhibited no signs of doing so. Perhaps an observation in Robert Gildea's book on France during the German Occupation of 1940-45 is apposite: 'Most French people followed Pétain for most of the Occupation, then de Gaulle. To abandon one for the other too soon was dangerous, to do it too late imprudent'. When it became clear that Germany was going to lose the war and that the Vichy regime would not last for ever, ingenious men, hitherto pillars of the regime, managed to withdraw in time to avoid being too intimately tied up with it, and made their peace with the Gaullists. There was a comparatively smooth transfer of power from the German-approved local authorities to the Gaullist approved ones; in a great many cases, the same functionary could continue in office. [47]

The analogy is clear. In 1688 the English ruling class was biding its time, fully appreciating that in such circumstances, timing was everything. As John Harington's witty epigram helpfully explained, 'Treason doth never prosper, what's the reason? For if it prosper, none dare call it treason'. Or, as Talleyrand was to observe more succinctly in the nineteenth century, 'Treason is a question of dates'.

Sir Edward Seymour, a Tory and the greatest electoral magnate in the west of England, was the first person of stature to visit William's headquarters in Exeter. Lord Colchester, Thomas Wharton, Edward Russell and the Earl of Abingdon followed. The Earl of Bath, the commander of the Plymouth

[47] Robert Gildea, *Marianne in Chains: In Search of the German Occupation,* 1940-45 (London, 2002), 42.

garrison, declared for William. The Earl of Danby and Lord Delamer rose in support of William in Yorkshire and Cheshire respectively. The Earl of Devonshire declared for William in the north Midlands.

As promised, many of the officers in James's army defected. On 24 November, three weeks after William's landing in England, John Churchill, who on the accession of James II in 1685, had been made a lieutenant general and effective commander-in-chief of James's army, met William at Axminster. Churchill had already given William assurances that he would in all circumstances stand by the Protestant religion. William welcomed Churchill with the words of King David in the Old Testament: 'If you be come peaceably unto me, my heart shall be knit unto you'. Churchill responded with the next verse: 'Thine we are, David, and on thy side, thou son of Jesse. Peace, peace be unto thee and peace be unto thy helpers, for thy God helpeth thee' (1 Chronicles 12:17-18). [48]

Schomberg, William's principal 'helper', is alleged to have greeted John Churchill with the infelicitous remark that 'he was the first lieutenant general he had ever heard of that had deserted his colours'. This seems highly improbable; not least because it would have been extremely tactless of Schomberg to make such an observation for mass defections from James's army were exactly what William desired. That was the purpose of William's manifesto to the army:

> We hope… that you will not suffer yourselves to be abused by a false Notion of Honour, but that you will in the first place consider what you owe to Almighty God and your Religion, to your Country, to yourselves and to your Posterity, which you as Men of Honour, ought to prefer to all private Considerations and Engagements whatsoever.[50]

If Schomberg did make the remark, his comment might be construed as akin to the pot calling the kettle black because arguably Schomberg himself had changed sides, not as a lieutenant general but as a marshal of France.

---

[48] John E. Wills, *1688: A Global History*, 181-3.
[49] Winston S. Churchill, *Marlborough: His Life and Times* (London: Folio Press, 1991), i, 232
[50] Churchill, *Marlborough*, i, 232.

Furthermore, Winston Churchill in his *Life of Marlborough* makes the interesting point that his great ancestor commissioned a portrait of Schomberg. It seems highly unlikely that a man would commission a portrait of someone who had insulted him.[51] William rewarded Churchill with the Earldom of Marlborough, membership of the Privy Council, confirmation of his military rank, and ultimately a succession of commands in Flanders and in Ireland.

Deserted by Churchill and many of his officers, James found himself unable to mount an effective military challenge to William. So William advanced on London unopposed and a demoralised James attempted to flee the country.[52] William later facilitated a second, successful escape, creating the political vacuum that William desired.

In inviting William to invade, the Tories, the Whigs and the Church of England had differing objectives and William himself had his own motives for accepting.[53] The Tories and the Anglican clergy wished to stop James undermining the Church of England but they had no desire to depose James

---

[51] Churchill, *Marlborough*, i, 232n.

[52] News of James's first flight reached William while he was dining with Schomberg. An eyewitness noted that William 'was very cheerful and could not conceal his satisfaction at the King's being gone'. Van der Zee, *William and Mary*, 262.

[53] Cruickshanks claims that William sought the Crown from the first. John Miller believes that William considered the possibility of becoming king, but interprets the evidence as suggesting that William would have been satisfied with less. In Miller's estimation, William's minimum aims were to secure Mary's claim to the succession and to secure a free Parliament which, he assumed, would force James to declare war on France and perhaps give him some say in the conduct of the war. Horace Walpole, the literary son of Sir Robert Walpole, opined: 'I do not doubt but King William came over with a view to the crown. Nor was he called upon by patriotism, for he was not an Englishman, to assert our liberties. No; his patriotism was of a higher rank. He aimed not at the crown of England for ambition, but to employ its forces and wealth against Louis XIV for the common cause of the liberties of Europe. The Whigs did not understand the extent of his views, and the Tories betrayed him. He has been thought not to have understood us; but the truth was he took either party as it was predominant, that he might sway the parliament to support his general plan.' Cruickshanks, *The Glorious Revolution*, 25; John Miller, *The Glorious Revolution* (London, 1983), 13-14; Horace Walpole, Letter to William Mason, c. 1792, quoted in Justin Wintle and Richard Kenin, *The Penguin Concise Dictionary of Biographical Quotation* (Harmondsworth, 1981), 649.

since they believed he was the Lord's anointed and their divinely ordained monarch. The Whigs, on the other hand, wished to depose James II and to place limits on the powers of the Crown. Ordinary people, drawing on a distrust of Roman Catholicism going back to the Marian persecutions of the 1550s – recently reinforced by the fate of the Huguenots in France and the bloody suppression of the West Country after Monmouth's rebellion – mistrusted James II for his attachment to Roman Catholicism.

The Tories argued for James's return as a limited King, or for a regent to rule for him or for Mary to rule as Queen. William wanted rid of James because he regarded him as an ally of Louis XIV of France. The Convention Parliament, summoned in January 1689, had a Whig majority and subscribed to the Whig formula, more congenial to William, which construed James's flight to France as abdication, declared the throne vacant, and offered it, with an accompanying Declaration of Rights, to William and Mary as joint sovereigns. While the limits placed on the Crown by the Bill of Rights were less than the Whigs desired, it nevertheless pronounced the suspending power – the very definition of arbitrary rule – illegal and forbade a standing army without parliamentary approval. The latter requirement made Parliament a regular and permanent feature of political life. The Declaration also barred Roman Catholics from the succession to the throne. William and Mary were proclaimed as joint sovereigns in February and crowned on 21 April 1689. In Scotland the Revolution went further. There James was actually deposed, bishops were abolished and Presbyterianism was restored.[54]

William and Mary and a grateful nation expressed their appreciation to Schomberg for his contribution to the success of William's great enterprise. He became a naturalized Englishman in April 1689 and in May was created Duke of Schomberg (as well as Baron of Teyes, Earl of Brentford, and Marquess of Harwich). Following the coronation of William and Mary Schomberg was made a Knight of the Order of the Garter.

---

[54] On 4 April 1689 the Scottish Convention voted that James had not abdicated, but 'by doing acts contrary to law' had forfeited his right to the Crown. The Scottish Convention also condemned prelacy as 'a great and insupportable grievance'. Cruickshanks, *The Glorious Revolution,* 49.

Parliament also made him a gift of £100,000 to compensate him for the loss of his substantial confiscated French property. Privately, William expressed doubts whether Schomberg had fully earned so much but arguably Schomberg paid in full for the honours and patronage bestowed upon him with his life at the Boyne.[55]

The Death of Schomberg, Mural at the Reivers House, Kilkeel (courtesy of the Schomberg Society)

[55] John Carswell, *Descent on England,* 227. However, Schomberg would appear to have continued to enjoy royal favour. Churchill quotes the Jacobite exile General Dillon, who was a page at the court of William and Mary at the time, recalling in 1729 that 'he never saw English noblemen dine with the Prince of Orange, but only the Duke of Schomberg who was always placed at his right hand and his Dutch general officers. The English noblemen that were there stood behind the Prince of Orange's chair but were never admitted to eat and sit'. Churchill, *Marlborough,* i, 266.

James receives news of William's arrival

5 : BACKGROUND TO SCHOMBERG'S IRISH CAMPAIGN

Even before James II arrived at Kinsale on 12 March 1689,
William III, in an address to his English Parliament on 8 March,
spoke of 'the deplorable condition of Ireland', attributing it to
'the zeal and violence of the Popish Party there' and 'the assistance
and encouragement they have from France'.

He advised that a very considerable force, 'not less than 20,000 horse and foot', would be required to bring Ireland under control.[56] By mid March 1689 the House of Commons voted William £1,200,000 a year but this figure was arbitrarily arrived at, without serious consideration or investigation of what the King's actual needs were. Since it was insufficient to meet the Crown's needs in peacetime, it was wholly inadequate to meet the expenditure which military intervention in Ireland would incur. William was also extremely reluctant to commit troops to Ireland because he feared a Jacobite uprising in England. Furthermore, although the Scottish Convention Parliament had strongly supported him, William was also greatly concerned about the strength of Jacobite sentiment in Scotland, especially in the Highlands.

However, the delay in addressing events in Ireland, especially the increasingly desperate plight of the beleaguered defenders of Londonderry, occasioned mounting criticism of the Government. John Evelyn, the celebrated diarist, noted that 'the new king' was 'much blamed for neglecting Ireland' and allowing it to be 'ruined by Tyrconnell and the popish party'.[57] At beginning of July MPs were extremely angry that Ireland was 'overrun by [His] Majesty's declared enemies the French in conjunction with Irish rebels' and they wanted to know who was responsible for this state of affairs and why nothing was being done about it.[58]

---

[56] Robert Shepherd, *Ireland's Fate: The Boyne and After* (London, 1990), 52-3.
[57] Shepherd, *Ireland's Fate*, 63
[58] Shepherd, *Ireland's Fate*, 63.

Against this backdrop of mounting criticism, in mid July Schomberg was eventually appointed to command a Williamite expedition to Ireland. Throughout William's reign it has been observed that he preferred to employ Dutchmen and Huguenots in key positions. In *Britain and the World* (1980) J.R. Jones offered an interesting explanation for William's preference for his European associates:

> This was not primarily a matter of trust; he chose to ignore the secret 'insurance policy' connections which many (for example, Marlborough, Godolphin and Shrewsbury) maintained with the exiled James. Rather, William knew how ignorant and inexperienced were his English ministers, generals and diplomats, few of whom had any real appreciation of the difficulties and complexities of the business of waging a general European war. By employing personal associates of many years' standing – Portland, Athlone, Schomberg, Galway, Rochford – William created the impression that he retained prejudices against Englishmen, whereas his principal reason was that he needed men who would never question his orders. During the Restoration period few leading English politicians had developed the habit of obedience... [59]

The fact that Schomberg was unable to carry out William's orders to the letter and meet his, perhaps unrealistic, expectations was to be the source of great irritation to William.

Schomberg arrived at Chester on 20 July and planned to join forces with Major-General Kirke at the mouth of the Foyle. However, there were further delays caused by the lack of troops and equipment and by the lack of ships to transport them both to Ireland.[60] Much of the blame for this may be laid

[59] J.R. Jones, *Britain and the World* (Glasgow, 1980), 135.
[60] Interestingly, Walter Harris alleged: 'The Duke proposed not to wait for the transports, but to march the forces directly to Port Patrick in Scotland, from whence it was about a few hours passage into Ireland'. Harris continued by proffering an interesting counterfactual: 'Had this advice been pursued, it would probably have saved two or three months, and thereby prevented the rebellion of Dundee, relieved Londonderry, and hindered King James from forming so strong an army, and the French from landing in Ireland'. Unfortunately, these claims do not survive a moment's careful scrutiny of the chronology. Walter Harris, *The History of the Life and Reign of William-Henry, Prince of Nassau and Orange, Stadholder of the United Provinces, King of England, Scotland, France and Ireland, etc* (Dublin, 1749), 244. Reinforcements later in the season were frequently shipped from Scotland. Kenneth Ferguson, 'The Organisation of King William's Army in Ireland', *Irish Sword*, xviii, no. 70, 1990, 66. Three regiments of cavalry and one of infantry arrived from Scotland in October. Ferguson, 'The Organisation of King William's Army in Ireland', 66n.

at the door of Henry Shales, Chief Commissary to the army. Shales had been an enthusiastic Jacobite and probably remained an unreconstructed one. Moreover, he was corrupt and had no motivation to be efficient. Macaulay conveys something of the impact of Shales's malign politics and corruption on Schomberg's expedition:

> The beef and brandy which he furnished were so bad that the soldiers turned from them with loathing: the tents were rotten: the clothing was scanty: the muskets broke in the handling. Great numbers of shoes were set down to the account of the government: but, two months after the Treasury had paid the bill, the shoes had not arrived in Ireland. The means of transporting baggage and artillery were almost entirely wanting. An ample number of horses had been purchased in England with public money, and had been sent to the banks of the Dee. But Shales had let them out for harvest work to the farmers of Cheshire, had pocketed the hire and had left the troops in Ulster to get on as they best might.[61]

Flintlock musket, c.1690

Unhappily, Schomberg was saddled with a further serious problem. Quite apart from William's anxiety about the security of his position in England and Scotland, he had no great confidence in the loyalty of the regular English army. He regarded many of its officers as politically suspect. As they had betrayed James II, they were equally capable of betraying him. So William despatched the regular English army to the continent. Therefore a new army was raised for service in Ireland but the corollary of this was that these new troops had no military training worthy of the name. Macaulay offers the following commentary on the inexperience of the bulk of Schomberg's army:

[61] Macaulay, *History of England,* iii, 325.

Unfortunately almost all those English soldiers who had seen war had been sent to Flanders. The bulk of the force destined for Ireland consisted of men just taken from the plough or the threshing floor. [62]

However, a brigade of excellent Dutch troops, commanded by Count Solms, and four Huguenot regiments, three infantry and one cavalry, raised by the Marquess of Ruvigny, stiffened Schomberg's force.

Happily, in the interval between Schomberg's appointment to command the expeditionary force to Ireland and his departure, the situation throughout the British Isles had been transformed by events at the end of July 1689. On 28 July the *Mountjoy* broke the boom and brought to a close the 105-day-long siege of Londonderry.[63] On 30 July the Enniskillen men commanded by Colonel Wolseley defeated a superior Jacobite force under Viscount Mountcashel at

---

[62] Macaulay, *History of England,* iii, 314. A number of famous British regiments have their origins in the force raised for Schomberg's expedition to Ireland, notably the 22nd, 23rd and 24th Regiments of Foot. Originally they were raised in 1689, taking the names of their colonels, as the Duke of Norfolk's Regiment of Foot, Lord Herbert's Regiment of Foot and Dering's Regiment of Foot. They are better known today as the Cheshire Regiment, the South Wales Borderers (amalgamated in 1969 with the Welch Regiment to form the Royal Regiment of Wales) and the Royal Welch Fusiliers respectively. The Royal Welch Fusiliers is the only regiment in the British Army, with the exception of the Gurkhas, to employ a language other than English as the language of command, Welsh being the first language of many members of the regiment. During the Great War more than one battalion used Welsh on a regular basis. In Burma, in the Second World War, troops used Welsh to conceal their intentions from the Japanese. In 1995 the 1st Battalion used Welsh in Bosnia. 'Welch' is the old English way of spelling 'Welsh'. Throughout the years both forms have been used and during the Boer War and the Great War the official spelling was 'Welsh'. Army Order No. 56 of 1920 finally confirmed that the official spelling should be 'Welch'. 'To Toby Purcell, his spurs and the Boyne', the regimental toast of the Royal Welch Fusiliers, commemorates an incident at the Battle of the Boyne. Purcell, the regiment's second-in-command, was the first member of the regiment to cross the Boyne on 1 July 1690. Purcell's spurs were worn by successive seconds-in-command until they were lost in a fire at Montreal in 1842. Tobias (Toby) Purcell received his commission as colonel of the regiment on 26 October 1691. His commission, signed by William III, may be viewed on the web at www.gtj.org.uk/item.php?lang=en&id=25233&t=1 The Cheshire Regiment's website records that the regiment in its first campaign 'proceeded with an army, under General Schomberg, to Ireland, where it took part in the siege and capture of Carrickfergus. In the following year it was present at the Battle of Boyne, and in 1691 at the capture of Athlone and the Battle of Aughrim'. http://web.ukonline.co.uk/ewh.bryan/Cheshire-1.htm Oral information from Mr Howard Massey of Portadown and Mr Tommy Irwin of Wrexham.

Newtownbutler. In Scotland on 27 July
the Williamite cause suffered a
temporary set back at Killiecrankie
at the hands of a Highland army but,
more significantly, Viscount (better
known as 'Bonny') Dundee, the
charismatic Scottish Jacobite leader,
was mortally wounded in the battle.
Without Dundee's leadership the
Highland army, rent by clan
rivalries, started to disintegrate
and it was defeated a month later
at Dunkeld. The relief of Londonderry
and the Enniskillen men's victory at
Newtownbutler meant that there was no
immediate prospect of Ireland serving as a
stepping stone from which James could mount
an effective challenge to regain his lost English and Scottish thrones.
Furthermore, the death of Dundee and the Williamite victory at Dunkeld
on 21 August meant that the prospect of Scotland assisting James to regain
the English throne was also diminishing.

'Bonny' Dundee

[63] The Williamite relief force, commanded by Major-General Kirke, arrived in Lough Foyle on 13
June 1689 but made no attempt to relieve Londonderry because of the boom. Kirke's inactivity
incurred the wrath of Schomberg who wrote to Kirke on 3 July 1689 that his excuse for not
attempting to relieve the city was 'no otherwayes grounded than upon supposition that it is
uncertain whether the Boom and chain that are said to be laid acrosse the river can be broken or
the Boates that are reported to be sunck past over'. Kirke was ordered to find out the truth of the
matter 'by sending intelligent persons to view the places; and to get the best light they can of the
matter and to consult the Sea Officer whether it may not be possible to break the boom and chain
and to passe with the Ships, and that you attempt the doing of it for the reliefe of the town'. Some
readers may discern a parallel between Schomberg's irritation at Kirke's inactivity in Lough Foyle
in the summer of 1689 and William's indignation at Schomberg's failure to advance beyond
Dundalk in the autumn of 1689. Patrick Macrory, *The Siege of Derry* (London, 1980), 306-7.

Schomberg's Campaign in Ireland 1689 - 1690

1. **28 July 1689** - Relief of Londonderry.
2. **30 July 1689** - Enniskillen men defeat Jacobites.
3. **13 August 1689** - Schomberg lands at Groomsport.
4. **17 August 1689** - Schomberg enters Belfast.
5. **20 August 1689** - Schomberg lays seige to Carrickfergus; Carrickfergus surrenders 28th August 1689.
6. **2 September 1689** - Schomberg leaves Belfast and heads south.
7. **7 September - early November** - Schomberg's army camps here and suffers heavy losses from exposure and sic
8. **14 September 1689** - James II advances beyond Ardee but Schomberg declines his challenge.
9. **Winter 1689/1690** - Schomberg winters in Lisburn.
10. **14 May 1690** - Charlemont surrenders to Schomberg.
11. **1 July 1690** - Battle of the Boyne.

6: SCHOMBERG'S CAMPAIGN IN IRELAND

On 12 August 1689, following the relief of Londonderry, Schomberg set sail for the east coast of Ulster, with a convoy of five warships and 80 transports. The next day Schomberg's force was able to land unopposed at Groomsport on the southern shore of Belfast Lough (although contemporaries would have called it Carrickfergus Lough, a commentary on the comparative unimportance of Belfast in the seventeenth century).

Schomberg's landing was unopposed because Brigadier Maxwell, a Scottish Jacobite, decided that discretion was the better part of valour and withdrew his modest force of 500 men to Newry. Having secured his bridgehead, Schomberg's army, on 17 August, marched to Belfast where they were rapturously received by the town's Protestant inhabitants.

Schomberg then made the capture of Carrickfergus on the northern shores of Belfast Lough, the principal Jacobite stronghold in eastern Ulster, his first priority. He invested the town on 20 August. A week later, after being subjected to bombardment by land and sea, Colonel Charles McCarthy Mor, the commander of the Jacobite garrison, surrendered to Schomberg on terms.

Schomberg had immense difficulty in restraining the local Ulster-Scots population from violating the terms of surrender and wreaking revenge on the Jacobite garrison as they marched out of the Norman castle and the town:

> The Countrey people were so inveterate against them (remembering how they had served them some days before) that they stript most part of the Women, and forced a great many Arms from the men; and took it very ill that the Duke did not order them all to be put to Death, notwithstanding the Articles: but he knew better things; and so rude were the *Irish Scots* [sic], that the Duke was forced to ride among them, with his Pistol in his hand, to keep the *Irish* from being murdered. [64]

By the end of August a force of some 20,000 Williamite troops had been assembled in Ireland and further reinforcements would follow in September. Unfortunately, however, Schomberg did not wait for either these or his provisions or transport wagons. He gave orders for his supply ships to put in at Carlingford Lough and left Belfast on 2 September, marching south towards Newry and Dundalk. Schomberg's army advanced through territory laid desolate by Berwick, one of James II's illegitimate sons and an able soldier. Berwick's strategy prevented Schomberg's army purchasing provisions or even living off the land.

When Schomberg pitched camp just north of Dundalk in County Louth on 7 September, his supply ships had still not arrived in Carlingford Lough and his army was running seriously short of provisions. These facts may have had a significant bearing on Schomberg's otherwise almost inexplicable choice of campsite. The site was on marshy ground at the foot of hills and subject to heavy rainfall. His raw English troops had little appreciation of sanitation and were unwilling to learn. As a result the army was devastated by sickness, probably dysentery. 'Our men died like rotten sheep,' an English officer bitterly complained. A despairing Schomberg was obliged to conclude: 'The English nation is so delicately bred, that as soon as they are out of their own country, they die the first campaign'.[65]

Schomberg had never had troops under his command who were so ignorant, so untrained and so completely undisciplined as his English levies. They were also ill-equipped and lacking supplies through the corruption and incompetence of Shales and his subordinates, inherited from the previous regime.

[64] Story, *A True and Impartial History*, 10. Constantyn Huygens, accompanying William III to Ireland a year later, was much struck by the fact that the people who he and his royal master encountered around Carrickfergus refused to describe themselves as Irish: they vehemently insisted that they were Scots who had settled in Ireland. Van der Zee, *William and Mary*, 310. Eighteenth-century visitors were also struck by the tenacity of Scottish dialect, accent and manners in Ulster. See I. R. McBride, *Scripture Politics: Ulster Presbyterians and Irish Radicalism in the Late Eighteenth Century* (Oxford, 1998), 188.

[65] Van der Zee, *William and Mary*, 309.

[66] According to Lenihan, 'James II dejectedly considered abandoning Ireland altogether and if Schomberg had marched straight to Dublin he would have finished the war at a blow', *1690: Battle of the Boyne*, 72.

While Schomberg was encamped at Dundalk, James II's army was in Drogheda. Jacobite morale was at a low ebb, having experienced defeat at Londonderry and Newtownbutler.[66] Both qualitatively and quantitively, the Jacobite army left much to be desired. The Jacobites were genuinely perplexed by Schomberg's inactivity. Why was he not pushing on to Dublin? Rosen, the Baltic German who was a lieutenant-general in the French army, concluded that Schomberg's army 'wanted something necessary for their going forwards'. A deserter from Schomberg's army provided the missing detail: Schomberg's army lacked supplies and his troops were succumbing to illness. [67]

Emboldened by this knowledge, the Jacobites advanced as far as Ardee by 14 September. Two days later the Jacobites advanced beyond Ardee as far as the River Fane, some five miles south of Dundalk and on 17 September James brought his army within cannon-shot of Schomberg's army. George Story recounted:

> About nine a Clock in the morning (it being a very clear Sun-shine day) our Camp was alarmed; the Enemy display'd their Standard-Royal, and all drew out, both horse and foot, bringing along a very handsome field train. [68]

In other words, James deployed his troops for battle. For a fortnight the two armies were in close proximity.[69] Some of Schomberg's subordinates were keen to engage the Jacobites. According to Story, Schomberg's response was:

> 'Let them alone, we will see what they do.' He received several fresh accounts that the Enemy advanced, and always bid, 'Let them alone'. [70]

---

[67] J. G. Simms, *Jacobite Ireland, 1685-91* (London, 1969), 128.
[68] Story, *A True and Impartial History,* 22.
[69] In 1795 Lieutenant-General Keating, then a young subaltern at the outset of an illustrious military career, opined that James 'had Schomberg in a cul-de-sac, his retreat cut off, his army wasting by sickness, shut up in entrenchments, and James himself with a superior army in their front'. Keating believed that Schomberg's force could have been destroyed if James had had the resolution to attack. However, G. A. Hayes-McCoy contended that 'the Jacobites were little better than amateurs' and that 'they needed more time for organisation and training before they were ready to fight, and the delay at Dundalk earned it for them'. See G. A. Hayes-McCoy, 'The Boyne, 1690', *Irish Battles: A Military History of Ireland* (Belfast, 1990), 223.
[70] Story, *A True and Impartial History,* 22.

An exasperated William urged Schomberg to attack but Schomberg believed it would be sheer folly to risk a battle and invite defeat. Schomberg proffered various reasons for declining to give battle: his army lacked shoes, their food was inedible, and their pikes were so rotten that they disintegrated in their hands. By this stage his troops were dying in their hundreds of 'flux and fever'.[71] In early October Schomberg was extremely critical of his officers:

> I must tell your Majesty that if our Irish colonels were as able in war as they are to send to pillage the country, and not to pay the soldiers, your Majesty would be better served by them.[72]

These were not explanations likely to impress an impatient William.

On 6 October James withdrew to Ardee and at the beginning of November he moved from Ardee to winter quarters in Dublin. Similarly, Schomberg withdrew to winter in Lisburn, quartering his troops all over Ulster. Schomberg's withdrawal allowed Christopher Plunkett to retake Newry for the Jacobites, although it must have been a poor prize as the Duke of Berwick had burned the town to the ground a few months earlier as part of his scorched earth policy. Apart from some military activity in the environs of Belturbet in County Cavan, both sides largely suspended military operations over the winter months.[73] Schomberg resumed the campaigning season by expelling the Jacobites from Charlemont, their last remaining stronghold in Ulster, in May 1690.

---

[71] '…we lost nigh one half of the men that we took over with us'. Story, *A True and Impartial History*, 39. Lenihan reckons that Schomberg lost at least a third of his army without firing a shot. *1690: Battle of the Boyne*, 74.
[72] Van der Zee, *William and Mary*, 309.
[73] The Huguenot regiments were quartered as follows: La Caillemotte's in east Tyrone, La Mollonière's in Down, Cambon's in Down and Armagh, and the cavalry in Armagh and south Antrim. Harman Murtagh, 'Huguenot involvement in the Irish Jacobite War, 1689-91', Caldicott, Gough & Pittion (eds), *The Huguenots and Ireland*, 229.

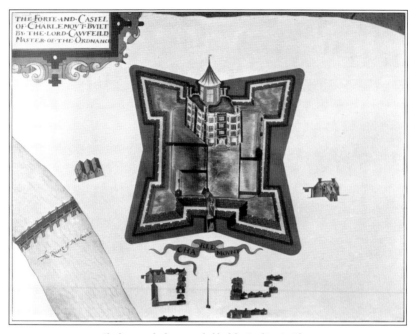

Charlemont, the last stronghold of the Jacobites in Ulster

King William III Statue, Carrickfergus Castle.
Unveiled by the Lord Lieutenant, County of Antrim, Captain R.A.F. Dobbs J.P. - 14th June 1990

7: WILLIAM'S INTERVENTION IN IRELAND

*For William the final months of 1689 had proved extremely frustrating.
He had entertained high hopes that Schomberg would have Ireland under
control by the end of the year. He had no hesitation in blaming Schomberg
for mishandling the campaign and confided to Bentinck that 'nothing
worthwhile would be done' unless he went to Ireland himself.* [74]

At the end of January 1690 in a speech to the House of Lords William signalled
his intention to intervene personally in Ireland:

> It is a very sensible affliction to me to see my good people burdened with taxes;
> but, since the speedy recovery of Ireland is, in my opinion, the only means to
> ease them, and to preserve the peace and honour of the nation, I am resolved to
> go thither in person, and, with the blessing of God Almighty, endeavour to reduce
> that kingdom. [75]

William was unable to turn his attention to Ireland immediately but the
preparations were set in motion for the campaign. In March 1690 the Williamite
army in Ireland was reinforced by the arrival in Belfast of seasoned Danish
cavalry and infantry. The Williamite cause was further strengthened by the
dispatch of English, German and Dutch troops in April and May. The military
build-up was accompanied by close attention to the resolution of problems of
logistics and supply, the source of so many of Schomberg's difficulties.

Eventually, on Wednesday 4 June 1690 William was able to set out for Ireland,
departing from Kensington and spending four days travelling to Chester.
Unfavourable winds delayed William's departure for three days so that it was on
Wednesday 11 June that he set sail from Hoylake with a fleet of almost 500
vessels escorted by Sir Cloudsley Shovell's squadron of warships. Fog and calm
caused further delay so that it was not until the afternoon of Saturday 14 June

---

[74] Simms, *Jacobite Ireland*, 134-5.
[75] Shepherd, *Ireland's Fate*, 79.

that William first caught sight of the Ulster coastline. He landed later in the day near Carrickfergus.

The same careful and meticulous planning for the forthcoming campaign was in evidence as that which preceded his arrival at Torbay two years earlier, for William brought with him a train of artillery from Holland, 450 bread wagons, 9,000 horses with fodder, £200,000 in cash and a further 15,000 troops. Every effort was made to avoid the problems which had beset Schomberg's army.

William and his party were greeted by Marshal Schomberg at Whitehouse, home of Sir William Franklin, husband of the Countess of Donegall. William then proceeded to Belfast in Schomberg's coach. William was still exasperated at Marshal Schomberg's failure to bring Ireland under control the previous year. Sir George Clarke, William's Secretary of State for the War in Ireland, recalled:

> I can't omit … to take notice of the little regard the king showed to that very great man, the old Duke of Schomberg: all the countenance and confidence was in the Dutch general officers, Count Solms, Mons[ieur] Scravemore etc., insomuch that the Duke, who commanded next under his Majesty, was not so much advised with about the march of the army, as he complained to me himself while we were in Belfast.[76]

William's impatience and anxiety to turn his attention to Europe was reflected in his observation, made while dining with Schomberg at Lisburn on 19 June, that he had not come to let the grass grow under his feet. He wasted no time in moving south. A fortnight later William reached the north bank of the River Boyne.

On 30 June, the eve of the Battle of the Boyne, William held a council of war in Mellifont Abbey. Marshal Schomberg, supported by some of the other generals, favoured an attack across the river at Oldbridge as a diversion, while the main army was to be concentrated upstream against the Jacobite left flank. On the other hand, Count Solms, the commander of the Dutch Guards and general of the infantry, advocated committing everything to a full frontal assault at Oldbridge. Schomberg's plan was the more imaginative and daring but William, still unforgiving of Schomberg's failure to bring Ireland under control the

[76] Shepherd, *Ireland's Fate*, 87.

previous year, was not inclined to heed his elderly marshal's advice. Instead, William opted for a compromise: the main assault would be at Oldbridge but a flanking attack upstream by approximately a third of the army would precede it. When the written orders confirming the decisions of the council of war were circulated to the various commanders that night, a somewhat miffed Schomberg, more accustomed to giving orders than receiving them, confessed to Sir George Clarke 'that it was the first order of the kind that was ever sent to him'.[77]

The battle was fought on Tuesday 1 July. The day started misty but soon cleared and brightened. Shortly after dawn, around 5:00 a.m., Meinhard Schomberg, Schomberg's 49-year old son who had celebrated his birthday the previous day, and James Douglas, the Scottish lieutenant general, set off upstream to the west with between 10,000 and 12,000 men to mount the flanking attack. The Jacobites had broken the bridge at Slane but a few miles downstream the Williamites found a ford at Rosnaree. A party of 800 Jacobite dragoons commanded by Sir Neil O'Neill, despite being massively outnumbered, vigorously defended the crossing until O'Neill was wounded. The Jacobites then retreated, allowing the Williamites to cross the river.

Observing, from the vantage point afforded by the hill of Donore, the movement of the Williamite force upstream, James formed the erroneous opinion that the entire Williamite army was similarly about to manoeuvre in the direction of Slane. Thus James ordered the bulk – possibly two-thirds – of his army, including his best French infantry regiments, to move towards Rosnaree. At Rosnaree the two forces confronted each other across a steep ravine with a marshy bottom. There was no fighting because the topography prevented the two forces coming to grips with each other.

William's diversionary tactics were proving to be astonishingly successful. The Jacobites had fatally weakened their position at Oldbridge and the greater part of their army had taken up position at Rosnaree, terrain over which fighting was impossible. Approximately a third of the smaller Jacobite army was left to confront two-thirds of William's larger army in the vital Oldbridge sector, which was where the bulk of the fighting was to take place.

---

[77] Peter Beresford Ellis, *The Boyne Water: The Battle of the Boyne, 1690* (London, 1976), 70.

William placed himself in charge of his left wing which was composed exclusively of cavalry. Schomberg was responsible for the infantry at the centre of the Williamite army who would bear the brunt of the fighting in the vital Oldbrige sector. Shortly after 10:00 a.m. Schomberg gave the word of command and three regiments of Dutch Blue Guards, who had marched down from the high ground under the cover of the ravine now known as King William's Glen, entered the river ten abreast and waded, waist-deep, across the ford. When they were halfway across they encountered heavy fire from Irish troops on the opposite bank. Nevertheless, the Dutch reached the southern bank and were followed by the Londonderry and Inniskilling regiments, commanded by John Mitchelburne and Gustavus Hamilton respectively. To their left were the two Huguenot regiments, whose commanders were the Comte de Caillemotte and François Cambon, a number of the English regiments and another Dutch regiment under the command of Count Nassau, William's cousin.

The Irish cavalry commanded by Tyrconnell in person, together with the Duke of Berwick, and Dominic Sheldon, an English Jacobite, repeatedly charged the hard-pressed Williamite infantry. William was very anxious as to the fate of his crack Dutch troops but they formed squares, presenting a *chevaux de frise* of bayonets, backed by volleys of musket fire. In this way they withstood and repulsed the waves of Jacobite horsemen.

The Huguenot regiments were also under severe pressure. Colonel Caillemotte, commander of one of the regiments, was mortally wounded. The Duke of Schomberg – readily recognisable by the blue ribbon of the Order of the Garter which he was wearing – rushed forward to rally the faltering Huguenots. [78] Pointing his sword towards the enemy, he addressed the Huguenots in French: *'Allons mes amis, rappelez votre courage et vos ressentiments, voilà vos persécuteurs.'* ('Recall your courage and your hurt, gentlemen; behold your

---

[78] Despite his German birth, Schomberg identified very strongly with the Huguenots: he was the colonel of a Huguenot cavalry regiment and – apparently – exhibited a degree of favouritism towards Huguenot units, a criticism of Schomberg echoed by George Story. Of Schomberg's seven or eight *aides-de-camp*, it was said that only one could speak English. Harman Murtagh, 'Huguenot involvement in the Irish Jacobite War, 1689-91', Caldicott, Gough & Pittion (eds), *The Huguenots and Ireland*, 226, 228. Story, *A True and Impartial History*, 85.

persecutors.') Those were his last words. As he spoke he was swiftly surrounded by a band of Irish cavalry. When the Irish horse withdrew Schomberg was found on the ground with two sabre wounds to his head and a bullet from a carbine lodged in his neck.[79] Jacobite accounts name the man who killed Schomberg as either Brian O'Toole, an Irish guardsman, or Sir Charles Take, an Englishman serving in Tyrconnell's regiment.[80] There is an alternative account of Schomberg's death which has him killed in the confusion of battle by a Huguenot who 'shot him into the throat, and down he did drop dead'.[81] The former account may be regarded as the traditional or the most widely accepted one. An obvious problem with the latter account is if Schomberg's wound was inflicted by a carbine he cannot have been the victim of 'friendly fire' because the carbine is a cavalry weapon and Williamite cavalry did not cross the Boyne until noon.[82]

The death of Schomberg made little impact on William. Sir George Clarke recorded that:

> The King had immediate notice of it by some of the Duke's aides-de-camp, but did not seem to be concerned, whether it was that he was not sorry or that his thoughts were employed about the regiment of the Dutch Guards, whom he apprehended in some danger from a body of Irish horse that was coming to attack them, I will not determine.[83]

Nevertheless, it may be observed that William was similarly unmoved by the almost simultaneous death of Dr George Walker as he rallied his fellow Ulstermen. Walker's bravery failed to impress William who is alleged to have observed, 'Fool that he was, what had he to do there?'

The Danish ambassador, in a despatch to Christian V of Denmark, provided his royal master with a significantly different explanation for William's reaction to Schomberg's death:

[79] Macaulay, *History of England,* iii, 486.
[80] Lenihan, *1690: Battle of the Boyne,* 182.
[81] Sir Robert Southwell in a letter, 2 July 1690, quoted in Jonathan Bardon, *A History of Ulster* (Belfast, 1992), 163.
[82] Lenihan, *1690: Battle of the Boyne,* 181.
[83] Shepherd, *Ireland's Fate,* 112.

[William] made a sign to say nothing about it, laying a finger to his lip. This was doubtless in order that the troops, who were very fond of him, should not be alarmed at the news. This sad intelligence, which afflicted the King more than he wished to show, hastened his crossing over to the other side of the river, so as to maintain the troops in the good order in which we saw them fighting. He went over about a quarter of an hour later. [84]

William subsequently paid generous tribute to the late Duke in his remarks to Meinhard Schomberg:

I deeply lament your father for I had a sincere friendship for him. I shall never forget his services or yours. I owe this day to you and will remember it all my life. You have lost much in your father. But I shall be your father, yours and your children's. [85]

However, because Meinhard Schomberg acquired a reputation as 'one of the hottest, fiery men in England', William would never give him any command where there was the prospect of action.[86]

While there is not total agreement as to the numbers killed on each side in the Battle of the Boyne, there is a broad consensus that, given that William had an army of 36,000 and James one of 25,000, losses on both sides were remarkably light: perhaps somewhere in the region of about 1,000 Jacobites and 500 Williamites. Of course, the modest number of casualties on both sides has prompted some commentators, among them Hilaire Belloc, to dismiss the battle as a mere skirmish.[87] However, of greater relevance, Macaulay in his great *History* noted, 'The slaughter had been less than on any battle field of equal importance and celebrity' and Schomberg's death constituted the death of 'the first captain in Europe':

---

[84] Ellis, *Boyne Water,* 102-3.
[85] Ellis, *Boyne Water,* 120.
[86] 'Meinhard Schomberg' in Stephens & Lee (eds), *DNB,* xvii, 925.
[87] Hilaire Belloc, *James the Second* (London, 1928).

To his corpse every honour was paid. The only cemetery in which so illustrious a warrior, slain in arms for the liberties and religion of England, could properly be laid was that venerable abbey, hallowed by the dust of many generations of princes, heroes and poets. It was announced that the brave veteran would have a public funeral at Westminster.[88]

Schomberg's remains were conveyed to St Patrick's Cathedral in Dublin and it was that cathedral rather than Westminster Abbey that became his final resting place. In death Schomberg was not accorded the tribute that might be thought to have been his due. His burial place remained unmarked until 1731 when the Dean and Chapter of St Patrick's Cathedral erected a black stone monument as a memorial. The Latin inscription was composed by Jonathan Swift, the most celebrated dean of St Patrick's, and recalls his observation that the Duke's family were too mean to record his burial there themselves. In translation, it reads:

> Beneath this stone lies the body of Frederick, Duke of Schomberg, who was killed at the Boyne AD 1690. The Dean and Chapter earnestly and repeatedly requested the Duke's heirs to undertake the erection of a monument in memory of their father. Long and often they pressed the request by letter and through friends. It was of no avail. At long last they set up this stone that at least you may know, stranger, where the ashes of Schomberg lie buried. The fame of his valour had greater power among strangers than had the ties of blood among his kith and kin. AD 1731. [89]

Schomberg Memorial, St. Patrick's Cathedral, Dublin

[88] Macaulay, *History of England,* iii, 490.
[89] Website of St Patrick's Cathedral, Dublin, www.stpatrickscathedral.ie

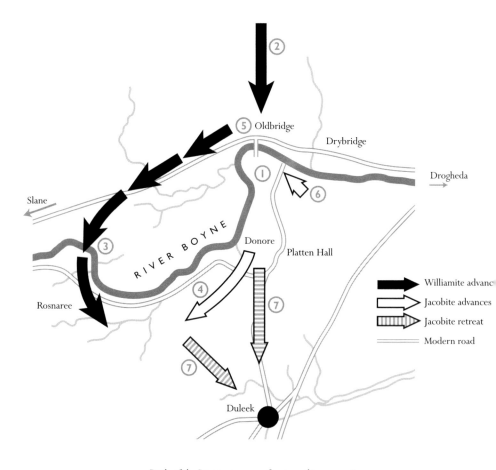

Battle of the Boyne: summary of major military operations

1. Jacobites occupy position at the bend of the river.

2. Williamites advance down King William's Glen.

3. As a feint, approximately one-third of the Williamite army, commanded by Meinhard Schomberg (Marshal Schomberg's son), advances towards Slane and crosses upstream at Rosnaree (Marshal Schomberg had advocated that this should be the main assault across the river).

4. Two-thirds of the Jacobite army moves south and west to counter the Williamite flanking movement.

5. Main Williamite assault starts at Oldbridge (Marshal Schomberg had advocated that this should be a feint whereas Count Solms, commander of the Dutch Blue Guard and the Williamite infantry, had wished this to be the one and only assault across the river).

6. The repeated Jacobite cavalry charges (during one of which Marshal Schomberg is killed).

7. Jacobites begin to retreat toward Dulleek.

8: Assessment

That Schomberg had a long and distinguished career as a soldier cannot be denied. Some might contend that Macaulay was guilty of hyperbole in describing Schomberg as 'the first captain in Europe'.[90]

However, with the Prince de Condé and Turenne both dead, if Schomberg was not 'the first captain in Europe', who was? Frederick William of Brandenburg, 'the Great Elector', was delighted to have Schomberg in his service. William of Orange clearly rated Schomberg very highly when he chose him as his second-in-command for the invasion of England. William's choice of Schomberg to command the expedition to Ireland was a further mark of confidence in the elderly marshal.

The Irish campaign of 1689 may be regarded as something of a stain on Schomberg's reputation. J.C. Beckett in *The Making of Modern Ireland 1603-1923* offered the following shrewd commentary on Schomberg's campaign in Ireland:

> He might, perhaps have safely pushed on to Dublin, for the Jacobites were weak and disheartened; but his army consisted mainly of raw recruits, he knew that a defeat might be politically disastrous to William's cause, and he preferred to wait for reinforcements. [91]

Schomberg's choice of site camp at Dundalk and his decision to remain there, seem almost inexplicable.[92]

---

[90] Macaulay, *History of England,* iii, 490.
[91] J.C. Beckett, *The Making of Modern Ireland, 1603-1923* (London, 1966), 144.
[92] Interestingly, Lenihan notes: 'Remarkably, Schomberg had presided over another death-camp earlier in his career. In the autumn of 1674 he stubbornly waited weeks on the Pyrenean frontier even though thousands of his men perished through dysentery and privation. In the end, he felt vindicated when the Spanish army pulled back, though his own army was so weakened that it could not advance until the following spring'. *1690: Battle of the Boyne,* 75.

Schomberg was undeniably beset by many difficulties and problems. The poor quality of his troops, the corruption of Henry Shales, and the inadequacy of his supply system were the principal cause of Schomberg's difficulties. In his *History* Macaulay mounted a robust defence of Schomberg:

> Wise and candid men said that he [Schomberg] had surpassed himself, and that there was no other captain in Europe who, with raw troops, with ignorant officers, with scanty stores, having to contend at once against a hostile army of greatly superior force, against a villainous commissariat, against a nest of traitors in his own camp, and against a disease more murderous than the sword, would have brought the campaign to a close without the loss of a flag or a gun. [93]

The House of Commons was sympathetic to Schomberg's plight. The English liked Schomberg because he was 'courteous and affable and yet had an air of grandeur and commanded respect'. The Commons attributed the failure of the campaign to 'the villainy of the Commissariat', and Herny Shales in particular. MPs were anxious to know who had recommended Shales for the important position of commissary general and why 'this creature of James' had been entrusted with supply of Schomberg's army. [94]

Privately, as we have seen, William blamed Schomberg for mishandling the campaign and confided to Bentinck that 'nothing worthwhile would be done' unless he went to Ireland himself; and so, at the end of January 1690, he signalled his intention to intervene personally in Ireland. However, John Childs in 'The Williamite War, 1689-1691' clearly distributes the blame for the fiasco far more widely and does not exonerate William himself. Childs condemns:

> the Treasury for incompetence; the king for failing to exercise executive authority over the army; the army for its suspect and divided loyalties and their ignorance of field conditions; Schomberg for tactical passivity; the House of Commons for their ignorance of the demands of modern war and their reluctance to vote sufficient funds; and Harbord [the army's paymaster] for greed and venality. [95]

---

[93] Macaulay, *History of England,* iii, 330.
[94] Macaulay, *History of England* iii, 384.
[95] John Childs, 'The Williamite War, 1689-1691' in Thomas Bartlett and Keith Jeffrey (eds) *A Military History of Ireland* (Cambridge, 1996), 196.

It is, thus, oversimplistic for Schomberg alone to be saddled with responsibility for the failure of the 1689 campaign.

Schomberg's views informed and shaped William's battle plan at the Boyne. The battle plan was most emphatically not that of Count Solms. Nor was it fully Schomberg's. William did incorporate Schomberg's plan for a diversion, although he inverted it. Whereas Schomberg advocated the attack across the river at Oldbridge as the diversion, while the main army was concentrated upstream against the Jacobite left flank, William opted for the main attack at Oldbridge with the attack on the Jacobite left upstream as the diversion. Nevertheless, the diversion was the key to William's success and the idea originated with Schomberg. It seems only proper to acknowledge that William's victory owed much to Schomberg and to what he had achieved, despite the problems that beset him, in the previous year.

William was bitter that Schomberg had not brought Ireland under control within six months but William left Ireland in September 1690 without achieving that goal either. William entrusted the task initially to Count Solms but because Solms was shortly afterwards recalled to England, the task ultimately fell to Baron von Ginkel. With the benefit of hindsight it can be seen that William, in entertaining high hopes of Schomberg having Ireland under control by the end of 1689, was being unrealistic. It was simply impossible to complete the task which Schomberg was given in mid July 1689 within less than six months.

Schomberg's courage at the Boyne cannot be questioned nor can he be accused of passivity in rushing forward to rally the faltering Huguenots. Pointing his sword towards the enemy, and rousing the Huguenots, the courage of the 'first captain in Europe', after about 60 years of soldiering, cost him his life.

Schomberg McDonnell, fifth son of the 5th Earl of Antrim

APPENDICES

APPENDIX A: A note on Schomberg McDonnell

While many are named 'William' in honour of the Prince of Orange, few are named in honour of Schomberg. Schomberg McDonnell, the fifth son of the 5th Earl of Antrim, is a conspicuous and interesting exception. Schomberg McDonnell was born on 22 March 1861 at Glenarm Castle and was educated at Eton and Oxford.[96]

In 1888 the 3rd Marquess of Salisbury, the Conservative Prime Minister and Foreign Secretary, appointed McDonnell as his principal private secretary, a position which he held almost continuously during Lord Salisbury's premierships. McDonnell was a family friend of the Cecils, having been best man at Viscount Cranborne's wedding in May 1887.[97] Salisbury described the work as 'interesting and not too hard'.[98] McDonnell had wisdom and tact before his 26 years, and as Salisbury's *homme d'affaires* he gradually became indispensable to 'The Chief'.[99]

Before the onset of the second Home Rule crisis, on 6 May 1892, Lord Salisbury delivered a controversial speech to the Grand Habitation of the Primrose League at Covent Garden in London. In his speech Salisbury alluded to the reign of James II and observed that Parliament had the right to govern the people of Ulster but it had no right to sell them into slavery. Salisbury said that he did not believe in the unrestricted power of parliaments any more than he believed in the unrestricted power of kings.

James II had stepped outside the spirit of the constitution and they knew how the people of Ulster had responded. Salisbury speculated that the 'people of Ulster', confronted by a similar abuse of power on the part of a parliament or a monarch, would demonstrate that they 'had not lost their sturdy love of freedom

[96] H.W.C. Davis & J. R.H. Weaver, *The Dictionary of National Biography, 1912-1921* (Oxford, 1927), 356-7.
[97] Andrew Roberts, *Salisbury: Victorian Titan* (London, 1999), 459.
[98] Roberts, *Salisbury*, 480.
[99] Roberts, *Salisbury*, 480.

nor their detestation of arbitrary power'.[100] Salisbury's speech was widely interpreted as meaning, 'Let Ulster rebel!' McDonnell denied that Lord Salisbury had used those words or any language which could sustain that interpretation. However, McDonnell was prepared to rebel and fight Home Rule.[101]

Created a KCB in 1902, Sir Schomberg was appointed in that year Secretary of the Office of Works. He occupied that position for ten years, retiring on urgent medical advice in September 1912. In 1911 he was awarded the GCVO.

Twice McDonnell volunteered for active military service. During the South African War (1899-1902) he served as a subaltern in the City of London Imperial Volunteers and, while serving in the field, he was gazetted a captain in the London Rifle Brigade.[102]

On the outbreak of the Great War in August 1914 he offered his services to Lord Kitchener, the newly-appointed Secretary of State for War, and was employed in the Intelligence Department. However, dissatisfied with a desk job, he sought and obtained an appointment in a battalion of the New Army. Although he had commanded a company of the London Rifle Brigade, he went to Chelsea for a three-week course of instruction prior to receiving his last commission.[103]

He was serving as a major with 5th Battalion Cameron Highlanders at the time of his death at the age of 54.[104]

The *Northern Whig* of 25 November 1915 reported that Lord Antrim's brother (i.e. Schomberg McDonnell) was 'wounded last Sunday in the trenches' and provided the following detail: 'It appears that he was struck by shrapnel, which inflicted a severe scalp wound, and his condition is regarded as grave.'

[100] Patrick Buckland, *Ulster Unionism and the Origins of Northern Ireland, 1886 to 1922* (Dublin, 1973), 15.
[101] Roberts, *Salisbury*, 589.
[102] Roberts, *Salisbury*, 760.
[103] Obituary, *Northern Whig*, 26 November 1915.
[104] Roberts, *Salisbury*, 828.

He had actually died two days previously on 23 November 1915. He is buried in Lijssenthoek Military Cemetry, 12 kilometres west of Ypres (or Ieper) town centre, on the Boescheepseweg, a road connecting Ieper to Poperinge. During the Great War Lijssenthoek was situated on the main communication line between the Allied military bases in the rear and the Ypres battlefields. Because Lijssenthoek was close to the front but out of range of most German field artillery, it was a natural place to establish casualty clearing stations. Lijssenthoek Military Cemetry was first used by the French 15th Hôpital d'Evacuation and in June 1915 it began to be used by British casualty clearing stations. [105]

---

[105] Commonwealth War Graves Commission website, www.cwgc.org

APPENDIX B: Schomberg, York County, Ontario[106]

The town of Schomberg, located in King Township, just north of Toronto, was originally named Brownsville after four industrious brothers who established a mill, a bank and a large farm in 1830. The settlement was founded in 1836.

By 1850 Brownsville had a population of slightly more than one hundred – people mainly from Ulster – and supported a tannery, a wagon shop, a tavern, a liquor store and two general stores. However, Brownsville did not possess its own post office. By 1861, Brownsville had overtaken the neighbouring and hitherto larger community of Lloydtown in size and qualified for this amenity.

Because there was already a Brownsville elsewhere in York County, the residents were obliged to come up with a new name for their growing community. The name Schomberg – 'after a hero who fell bravely fighting in the Battle of the Boyne' – was suggested by Thomas Roberts Ferguson, the Member of Parliament for South Simcoe, an Orangeman and the son-in-law of Ogle Gowan, the founder of Canadian Orangeism.

The construction of the Aurora and Schomberg Railway in 1902 dramatically transformed the local economy. While some local businesses benefited enormously many local craftspeople lost their jobs because machine-made goods brought in by the railway undercut the price of locally produced merchandise.

Like many Irish railways, the Aurora and Schomberg Railway was of comparatively short duration. Better roads and the expansion of truck transportation resulted in the closure of the railway in 1927.

Today Schomberg, with a population of approximately 3,000, might be most aptly described as a village serving a large farming community. There was once an Orange Lodge in the village, L.O.L. No. 736, but it no longer sits. However several lodges sit within a short drive from the village.

---

[106] Elizabeth McClure Gillham, *Early Settlements of King Township, Ontario* (Toronto, 1975) and oral information from Mr Alex Rough.

Views of Schomberg, York County, Ontario

FURTHER READING:

Thomas Bartlett & Keith Jeffrey (eds),
A Military History of Ireland (Cambridge, 1996).

J.C. Beckett,
The Making of Modern Ireland, 1603-1923 (London, 1966).

Eileen Black (ed),
Kings in Conflict: Ireland in the 1690s (Belfast, 1990) –
the Ulster Museum catalogue of the exhibition.

Robin Briggs,
Early Modern France, 1560-1715 (Oxford, 1977).

C. E. J. Caldicott, H. Gough & J-P Pittion (eds),
The Huguenots and Ireland: Anatomy of an Emigration
(Dun Laoghaire, 1987).

John Carswell,
*The Descent on England: A Study of the English Revolution of 1688
& its European Background* (London, 1969).

Winston S. Churchill,
Marlborough:His Life and Times (London: Folio Press, 1991).

Eveline Cruickshanks,
The Glorious Revolution (Basingstoke, 2000).

Richard Doherty,
The Williamite War in Ireland, 1688-1691 (Dublin, 1998).

R. Ernest Dupuy & Trevor N. Dupuy (eds),
Encyclopedia of Military History from 3500 BC to the present (1977).

J. H. Elliott,
Europe Divided, 1559-1598 (Glasgow, 1968).

J. H. Elliott,
Imperial Spain, 1469-1716 (Harmondsworth, 1963).

Peter Beresford Ellis,
The Boyne Water: The Battle of the Boyne, 1690 (London, 1976).

Robert Gildea,
Marianne in Chains: In Search of the German Occupation, 1940-45 (London, 2002).

Robin D. Gwynn,
Huguenot Heritage: The History and Contribution of the Huguenots in Britain (London, 1985).

Walter Harris,
The History of the Life and Reign of William-Henry, Prince of Nassau and Orange, Stadholder of the United Provinces, King of England, Scotland, France and Ireland, etc (Dublin, 1749).

Mary Howarth,
A Plain Man's Guide to The Glorious Revolution (London, 1988).

J. R. Jones,
Britain and the World, 1649-1815 (Glasgow, 1980).

S. J. Knox,
Ireland's Debt to the Huguenots (Dublin, 1959).

Padráig Lenihan,
1690: Battle of the Boyne (Stroud, 2003).

Lisburn Museum,
The Huguenots and Ulster, 1685-1985:Historical Introduction and Catalogue (Lisburn, 1985).

Anthony Livesey,
Battles of the Great Commanders (London, 1990).

Charles McConnell,
The Siege of Carrickfergus: The Story of Schomberg's Capture of the Town for William of Orange (Carrickfergus, 2000).

Thomas Babington Macaulay,
The History of England (London: Folio Press, 1986).

W. A. Maguire (ed),
*Kings in Conflict: The Revolutionary War in Ireland and its Aftermath,
1689-1750* (Belfast, 1990).

John Miller,
The Glorious Revolution (London, 1983).

David Ogg,
William III (London, 1956).

Geoffrey Parker,
Europe in Crisis, 1598-1648 (Glasgow, 1979).

Geoffrey Parker,
Spain and the Netherlands, 1559-1659 (Glasgow, 1979).

Geoffrey Parker (ed),
The Cambridge Illustrated History of Warfare (Cambridge, 1995).

Geoffrey Parker (ed),
The Thirty Years' War (London 1984).

Robert Shepherd,
Ireland's Fate: The Boyne and After (London, 1990).

J. G. Simms,
Jacobite Ireland, 1685-91 (London, 1969).

George Story,
A True and Impartial History of the Wars of Ireland (London, 1691).

John E. Wills,
1688: A Global History (London, 2001).

Henri & Barbara van der Zee,
William and Mary (London, 1973).

LIST OF ILLUSTRATIONS:

ACKNOWLEDGEMENTS:

Belfast Central Library and the Linen Hall Library were of immense value in researching this publication. The staff of both libraries were unfailing in their courtesy and were always anxious to be helpful. I am extremely grateful to them all.

I would also like to thank Winston Heaslip for his splendid guided tour of St Fethlimidh's Cathedral, Kilmore, County Cavan, and showing me George Story's grave.

Thanks are also due to Howard Massey, Portadown, and Tommy Irwin, Wrexham, for their interest in the composition of Schomberg's expedition to Ireland in 1689 and providing me with the story of 'Toby Purcell, his spurs and the Boyne', the regimental toast of the Royal Welch Fusiliers.

I am also grateful to Alex Rough, Bowmanville, Ontario, for his invaluable assistance with the origins of Schomberg, York County, Ontario.

I am deeply indebted to Roger Bradley and Mark Thompson for tracking down illustrations and to Mark Thompson for designing both the cover and layout.

Roger Bradley and Mark Thompson also shouldered all the responsibility of ensuring that the book had a smooth passage to the printing stage and beyond.

I would like to thank the members of the Educational Affairs Committee of the Grand Orange Lodge of Ireland for their support and encouragement.

This publication owes much to the advice and experience of John Erskine.

Such failings and errors which persist are my responsibility and mine alone.